MEGA STORMS

Discovery

Discovery

Front cover: ©2013 DCL, Shutterstock.com, Photodisc
Back cover: Shutterstock.com: Dariusz Kantorski, Arindambanerjee
Inside cover: Shutterstock.com: Emilia Ungur, Dariusz Kantorski
Photo credits:
Library of Congress: E.J. Frazier, Thompson, Montana, 42;
Photodisc: 3, 12, 13, 14, 15, 25, 40, 41, 42, 43, 48, 49, 50, 51, 52, 53, 55;
Thinkstock: 4, 5, 36, 37, 46, 47, 54, 55;
©2013 DCL: 6, 7, 8, 9, Mark Downey, 29; Peter Hurley, 14, 15;
Tommy Lorentsen, 24; Bedu Saini, 24;
NASA: NASA Planetary Photojournal, NASA/JPL-Caltech/Space Science
Institute, NASA/JPL-Caltech/MSSS;
NOAA: 8, 9, 10, 11, 38, 39, Lance Cpl., Ethan Johnson, U.S. Marine Corps, 26;
George E. Marsh, 38, 39; Steve Nicklas, NOS, NGS, 20;
Lance Cpl., Garry Welch, U.S. Marine Corps, 26;
USGS: Lynn Highland, 34, 35; Dave Wald, 34;
Shutterstock.com: 2009fotofriends, 48, 49; Action Sports Photography, 51; Giordano Aita, 50, 51;
Ugorenkov Aleksandr, 40, 41; Amidala76, 42; Aninticha, 28, 29, 30, 31; Arindambanerjee, 3, 30, 31;
Asianet-Pakistan, 3, 22, 23; Atomazul, 48; Beboy, 32, 33; Bertrand Benoit, 52, 53; Brandelet, 43; Brisbane, 32;
Michael D. Brown, 50; Charles Brutlag, 37; Sascha Burkard, 50, 51; Cholder, 38; CURAphotography, 18;
Dainis Derics, 20, 41; Doodle, 3, 48; Dustie, 10, 11; Ecco3d, 32; Guentermanaus, 44, 45; Matt Grant, 16;
James R. Hearn, 27, 54; Lim Yong Hian, 3, 18, 19; HomeArt, 54; Nataliya Hora, 44; John Huntington, 1; Jenny T, 54;
Glynnis Jones, 15; Josch, 36, 37; Julien_N, 40; Dariusz Kantorski, 28, 29; Konstantin Komarov, 17; Jonathan Lenz, 46;
LittleStocker, 55; Minerva Studio, 46; Robert Miramontes, 49; Mishella, 50; Modfos, 20; Byron W. Moore, 52;
Morrison, 35, 55; Iv Nikolny, 56; Anton Oparin, 14; Pictureguy, 47; George Allen Penton, 30;
Zacarias Pereira da Mata, 3, 18, 19; Catalin Petolea, 36; Mikhail Pogosov, 42, 43; Portokalis, 46; Rene Ramos, 19;
Daniel J. Rao, 23; Thomas Riggins, 43; Lisa S., 20, 21; R. Gino Santa Maria, 6; Semork, 16, 17; Todd Shoemake, 10, 11;
Solarseven, 3, 8, 9; Nigel Spiers, 56; Spirit of America, 28, 44; Pattie Steib, 13; Alexey Stiop, 6; Nikolajs Strigins, 32,
33; Sunshine Pics, 3; Emilia Ungur, 6, 7; Christian Vinces, 26, 27; Krivosheev Vitaly, 46, 47; Peter Weber, 36;
Yankane, 27; YexelA, 12; Gary Yim, 18; Andrey Yulov, 24, 25

Publications International, Ltd.

Published by
Louis Weber, C.E.O.
Publications International, Ltd.
7373 North Cicero Avenue
Lincolnwood, Illinois 60712

Ground Floor, 59 Gloucester Place
London W1U 8JJ
Customer Service:
1-800-595-8484 or customer_service@pilbooks.com

www.pilbooks.com

8 7 6 5 4 3 2 1

Manufactured in USA.

ISBN-13: 978-1-4508-7469-4
ISBN-10: 1-4508-7469-X

CONTENTS

MEGASTORMS
WHERE IS IT HAPPENING

**Prince William Sound
Alaska
Earthquake 1964**

**Rat Islands, Alaska
Earthquake 1965**

**Manicouagan Crater
Quebec, Canada**

**Laki V...
Iceland**

**Eyjafjallajökul
Volcano
Iceland 2010**

**Wellington,
Washington
Avalanche 1910**

**Northern Plains
Drought 1988**

**Tri-State
Tornado 1925**

**Johnstown, Pennsylvania
Flood 1889**

**Joplin
Tornado 2011**

**Storm of the
Century
Blizzard 1993**

**The Dust Bowl
Drought
1931-39**

**Hurricane
Super Storm
Sandy 2012**

**Fort Worth, Texas
Thunderstorm 1995**

**Hurricane
Katrina
2005**

**Seffner,
Florida
Sinkhole
2013**

**Haiti
Earthquake
2010**

**Nevado del Ruiz
Volcano 1985**

**Huascarán
Avalanche
1970**

**Chile
Earthquake
1960**

They're Getting Bigger

There is no place on Earth that is immune to storms and natural disasters. Whether it is an earthquake and tsunami in Japan, a tornado in Joplin, Missouri, or a fierce flood in Pakistan, Mother Nature is not shy about exercising her considerable muscle—often with devastating results.

Megastorms brings you some of the most dramatic displays of Mother Nature's force and fury.

Storm Key

 Tornado **Hurricane** **Cyclone** **Typhoon** **Flood** **Tsunami**

 Earthquake **Volcanic Eruption** **Landslide** **Drought** **Dust Bowl** **Blizzard** **Avalanche** **Sinkhole** **Thunderstorm** **Meteor**

Neva River Floods 1824

mes River & nds Floods 1099

White Friday Avalanche 1916

Messina, Italy Tsunami 1908

ount Vesuvius olcano 79 AD

Chelyabinsk, Russia Meteor 2013

Kamchatka, Russia Earthquake 1952

Pakistan Floods 2010

Daulatpur & Saturia, Bangladesh Tornado 1989

Sichuan Province Landslide 2008

Tohoku, Japan Tsunami 2011

Cyclone Bhola 1970

Cyclone Nargis 2008

Qattara Depression Egypt Sinkhole

Typhoon Bopha 2012

East Africa Drought 2011

& Africa s 2009

Congo Basin Thunderstorms

Indian Ocean Tsunami 2004

Mozambique Flood 2000

Mount Tambora Volcano 1815

Gosses Bluff Crater Northern Territory Australia

Woodleigh Crater Western Australia

Vredefort Crater Free State, South Africa

Acraman Crater South Australia

TORNADOES
TERRORS FROM THE SKY

It Sounded Like a Freight Train

Tornadoes are among nature's most violent, destructive storms. Most tornadoes develop inside severe thunderstorms, when a current of warm, moist air meets cool, dry air. A decrease in pressure at the center of the storm creates a rotating column of air called a vortex. Some tornadoes have a single vortex and others have multiple vortices rotating around a common center.

Tornadoes are given a rating on the *Enhanced Fujita (EF) scale*, which estimates wind speeds based damage.

EF0: wind gusts between 65-85 mph
EF1: wind gusts between 86-110 mph
EF2: wind gusts between 111-135 mph
EF3: wind gusts between 136-165 mph
EF4: wind gusts between 166-200 mph
EF5: wind gusts over 200 mph

Did you know?

Tornadoes rotate counterclockwise in the Northern Hemisphere and clockwise south of the equator.

World's Worst Tornadoes

Rank	Locations	Year	Fatalities
1	Daulatpur and Saturia, Bangladesh	1989	1,300
2	Madarganj to Mrizapur, Bangladesh	1996	700+
3	Missouri, Illinois, and Indiana	1925	695
4	Manikganj, Singair, and Nawabganj, Bangladesh	1973	681
5	Northeast suburbs of Dhaka, Bangladesh	1969	660
6	Valletta, Malta	1550s	600
7	Narail and Magura Districts, Bangladesh	1964	500
8	Sicily, Italy	1851	500
9	Madaripur and Shibchar, Bangladesh	1977	500
10	Belyanitsky, Ivanovo, and Balino, Russia	1984	400

Tornado Alley

Most tornadoes in the United States occur in the Deep South and in an area between the Rocky Mountains and the Appalachian Mountains known as Tornado Alley. The climate in this region helps spawn hundreds of tornadoes each year.

TERROR IN THE TRI-STATE

It Doesn't Get Any Worse Than This

The worst tornado in American history struck Missouri, Illinois, and Indiana without warning on March 18, 1925. The Tri-State Tornado destroyed thousands of structures and caused the confirmed deaths of 695 people, mostly in the town of Murphysboro, Illinois. The brick walls of the Longfellow School in Murphysboro caved in, killing 17.

The roof of the Mobile & Ohio Railroad shops and roundhouse buckled on 500 workers, killing 35 and injuring hundreds. The Blue Front Hotel collapsed, leaving many in the basement alive only to die when the hotel caught fire in the hours after the tornado.

Did you know?

The Tri-State Tornado holds the U.S. record for the longest path (219 miles) and duration (3.5 hours).

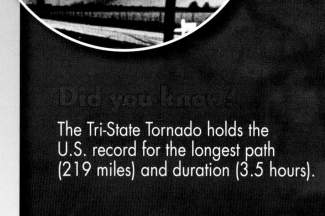

The tremendous force of the wind thrust this board through this plank.

Date: March 18, 1925

Locations: Illinois, Indiana, and Missouri

Category: EF5

Fatalities: 695

Damage: $16 million ($1.7 billion in today's dollars)

TEARING UP JOPLIN

Joplin's Path to Destruction

It was a hot Sunday afternoon on May 22, 2011, when a supercell thunderstorm spawned one of the deadliest tornadoes in U.S. history. The Joplin tornado's path was 22.1 miles long and up to one mile wide. It produced wind gusts greater than 200 miles per hour. The tornado intensified into an EF5 tornado as it moved into Joplin, Missouri, killing 158 people and injuring more than 1,000.

Trees were stripped of bark. Heavy trucks were picked up and thrown several blocks away. Nearly 7,000 homes were completely flattened or blown away.

Date: May 22, 2011
Location: Joplin, Missouri
Category: EF5
Fatalities: 158
Damage: $2.8 billion

Did you know?

The Joplin tornado was the costliest single tornado in U.S. history, with property damage totaling $2.8 billion.

HURRICANES
NATURE'S TANTRUMS

Batten Down the Hatches

Hurricanes form over warm seas and bring violent winds, heavy rains, and storm surges. These circular storms move around a low-pressure center. As hurricanes pass from sea to land, they can cause massive damage.

In August 2005, Katrina made landfall as a Category 3 hurricane. Katrina caused widespread destruction along the central Gulf Coast states. Cities such as Mobile, Alabama, Gulfport, Mississippi, and New Orleans, Louisiana, bore the brunt of Katrina's fury. Most of New Orleans was flooded in up to 20 feet of water.

Saffir-Simpson Scale

Category	Sustained Winds	Damage
1	74-95 mph	Minimal
2	96-110 mph	Moderate
3	111-129 mph	Extensive
4	130-156 mph	Extreme
5	157 mph or higher	Catastrophic

Did you know?

The Atlantic hurricane season runs from June 1st through November 30th.

Deadliest Hurricanes in U.S. History

Rank	Name	Year	Category	Fatalities
1	Great Galveston Hurricane	1900	4	8,000
2	Lake Okeechobee Hurricane	1928	4	2,500
3	Hurricane Katrina	2005	3	1,800
4	Cheniere Caminada Hurricane	1893	4	1,100 to 1,400
5	Sea Islands Hurricane	1893	3	1,000 to 2,000
6	Florida Keys Hurricane	1919	4	778
7	Georgia Hurricane	1881	2	700
8	Hurricane Audrey	1957	4	416
9	Great Labor Day Hurricane	1935	5	408
10	Last Island Hurricane	1856	4	400

SUPER STORM SANDY

Ripping Through the East Coast

Sandy developed in the Caribbean and made landfall as a Category 1 hurricane in Jamaica. Sandy gathered steam and hit Cuba as a Category 3 hurricane with winds of 115 miles per hour.

On October 29, 2012, Sandy struck the United States as a post-tropical hurricane, bringing massive destruction and flooding to the East Coast and Mid-Atlantic states. New Jersey and New York suffered the most devastating effects. Sandy killed at least 147 people directly and another 138 indirectly, left thousands homeless, caused billions of dollars in damage, and cut power to nearly eight million people.

Did you know?

Storm names for the Atlantic Basin are typically reused every six years, but Sandy has been retired from the official list because of the extreme destruction the storm caused.

Dates: October 22-31, 2012

Locations: Caribbean Islands, Eastern United States, and Canada

Category: 3

Fatalities: 285 total

Damage: $75 billion

CYCLONES
HURRICANE'S SISTERS

Nargis Annihilation

Cyclone Nargis made landfall in Myanmar (Burma) on May 2, 2008. The Category 3 cyclone ravaged the Ayeyarwady Delta region. Around 84,500 people were killed and 53,800 went missing. Damage was most severe in the Delta region, also known as the country's rice bowl, where the effects of extreme winds were compounded by a 12-foot storm surge. Nargis was the worst natural disaster in the history of Myanmar, and the most devastating cyclone to hit Asia since 1991.

Did you know?

Hurricanes, cyclones, and typhoons are all the same type of storm, but have different names in different places. Cyclones occur in the South Pacific and Indian Ocean.

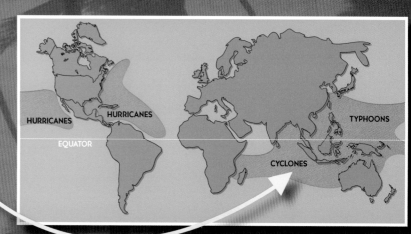

HURRICANES

HURRICANES

EQUATOR

TYPHOONS

CYCLONES

Killer Cyclones

Rank	Name	Locations	Year	Fatalities
1	Bhola Cyclone	East Pakistan (now Bangladesh)	1970	500,000
2	Hooghly River Cyclone	India and Bangladesh	1737	300,000
3	Coringa Cyclone	India	1839	300,000
4	Backerganj Cyclone	Bangladesh	1584	200,000
5	Great Backerganj Cyclone	Bangladesh	1876	200,000
6	Chittagong Cyclone	Bangladesh	1897	175,000
7	Cyclone 02B	Bangladesh	1991	140,000
8	Great Bombay Cyclone	India	1882	100,000
9	Cyclone Nargis	Myanmar	2008	84,500
10	Calcutta Cyclone	India	1864	60,000

Dates: May 2-3, 2008
Location: Myanmar
Category: 3
Fatalities: 84,500
Damage: $4 billion

TYPHOONS
CYCLONE'S SISTERS

Don't Mess With Miss Bopha

Bopha was the strongest typhoon to ever strike the southern Philippine island of Mindanao. Typhoon Bopha, known locally as Pablo, first hit the tiny island nation of Palau before making landfall on the east coast of Mindanao on December 4, 2012, as a Category 5 super typhoon. Winds up to 161 miles per hour and torrential rains caused floods and landslides. Bopha leveled entire villages, left thousands homeless, and caused major damage to critical infrastructure and agriculture. In all, 6.2 million people were affected by the typhoon.

Top Typhoon Records

Deadliest Typhoon	Haiphong Typhoon - 1881	300,000 fatalities
Maximum Wind Speed	Typhoon Nancy - 1961	213 mph
Longest Lasting Typhoon	Typhoon Page - 1990	26 days
Largest Typhoon	Typhoon Tip - 1979	1,380 mi diameter
Most Active Pacific Typhoon Season	1964	19 typhoons, 7 super typhoons

Did you know?

An average of 20 typhoons hit the Philippines each year.

Dates: November 25 - December 9, 2012

Locations: The Philippines, Micronesia, and Palau

Category: 5

Fatalities: 1,067

Damage: $1.04 billion

FLOODS
WATER ON A RAMPAGE

It Just Kept Raining

The main causes of flooding are excessive rains, the overflow of rivers and lakes, and storm surges. Flash floods, which can occur suddenly as the result of heavy rainfall, are the most lethal.

DANGER
Flooded Area
STAY OUT

Some of the deadliest floods in world history have happened when the Huang He (Yellow) River in China surpassed its banks. The silt that gives the river its yellow tint and name can pile up until the river is higher than the surrounding land. The 1931 Yellow River flood killed more than one million people and left 80 million people homeless.

THIRD STREET, WILLIAMSPORT, PA. DURING THE FLOOD.

Did you know?

The deadliest flood in American history occurred in Johnstown, Pennsylvania, in 1889. The flood killed 2,209 people and was the result of a dam failure and heavy rainfall.

World's Fiercest Floods

Rank	Name/Locations	Year	Fatalities
1	Huang He (Yellow) River flood, China	1931	1 to 3.7 million
2	Huang He (Yellow) River flood, China	1887	900,000 to 2 million
3	Huang He (Yellow) River flood, China	1938	500,000 to 900,000
4	Huang He (Yellow) River flood, China	1672	300,000
5	Typhoon Nina-Banqiao Dam failure, China	1975	230,000
6	Yangtze River flood, China	1931	145,000
7	Thames River & Netherlands floods, Netherlands & England	1099	100,000
8	St. Lucia's flood, The Netherlands	1287	50,000
9	The Neva River flood, Russia	1824	10,000
10	St. Elizabeth's flood, The Netherlands	1421	2,000 to 10,000

MEGAMONSOON PAKISTAN

Water, Water Everywhere

Monsoons are seasonal winds that shift direction and cause excessive rainfall. Monsoon season can be a welcome reprieve from drought conditions in many areas. But monsoons can also inflict major damage.

In July 2010, Pakistan experienced unprecedented monsoon flooding. A reported 10,860 different villages were completely inundated by floodwaters when parts of the Indus and Swat rivers swelled to more than 10 to 20 times their normal heights. Water exceeded 18 feet throughout flooded areas of Pakistan. More than 1.89 million homes were damaged or destroyed.

Did you know?

Islamabad, Pakistan, holds the country's record for most rainfall in one 24 hour period. In 2001, a record 24.4 inches of rain fell in one day.

Dates: July - August, 2010
Location: Pakistan
Fatalities: 1,645
Damage: $10 billion

TSUNAMIS
WAVES OF DESTRUCTION

Giant Walls of Water

A tsunami is a series of waves triggered by an earthquake, volcanic eruption, landslide, or meteorite. Waves radiate outward from the source and can spread across an entire ocean. The speed at which tsunamis travel depends on ocean depth. A tsunami in the deep ocean can travel more than 500 miles per hour. As a tsunami approaches land and shallow water, the waves slow down and grow higher.

On December 26, 2004, an underwater earthquake in the Indian Ocean produced the deadliest tsunami in history. Within 10 minutes of the earthquake, tsunami waves began pounding nearby shores. Banda Aceh, Indonesia, was struck with tsunami waves 65 feet high, which carried debris nearly two miles inland. The Indian Ocean tsunami killed more than 230,000 people in 14 countries.

Did you know?

Tsunami waves can be as long as 60 miles and as far apart as one hour.

Top 10 Tsunamis

Rank	Location	Year	Cause	Fatalities
1	Indian Ocean	2004	Earthquake	230,000
2	Messina, Italy	1908	Earthquake	70,000
3	Lisbon, Portugal	1755	Earthquake	50,000
4	South China Sea	1782	Earthquake	40,000
5	Krakatau, Indonesia	1883	Volcano	36,500
6	Enshunada Sea, Japan	1498	Earthquake	31,000
7	Tokaido-Nankaido, Japan	1707	Earthquake	30,000
8	Sanriku, Japan	1896	Earthquake	26,300
9	Northern Chile	1868	Earthquakes	25,674
10	Tōhoku, Japan	2011	Earthquake	19,300

TSUNAMIQUAKE JAPAN

An Earthquake Gives Birth to a Tsunami

One of the strongest earthquakes ever recorded struck off the northeastern coast of Japan's largest island, Honshu, on March 11, 2011. The magnitude 9.0 earthquake triggered a series of tsunami waves that traveled at speeds approaching 500 miles per hour, rose up to 133 feet high, and penetrated up to six miles inland. The disaster devastated many of Japan's Pacific coastal communities. Hundreds of thousands of people were killed, injured, or went missing. Thousands more were displaced.

Did you know?

Damage from the 2011 earthquake and tsunami totaled $305 billion, making it the costliest natural disaster in world history.

TSUNAMI EVACUATION ROUTE

Date: March 11, 2011
Location: Japan
Magnitude: 9.0
Fatalities: 19,300
Damage: $305 billion

And the Walls Came Tumbling Down

The largest earthquake in history shook southern Chile on May 22, 1960. The magnitude 9.5 earthquake killed 1,655, injured 3,000, and left 2 million people homeless. Seismic waves shook the entire planet for days.

Earthquakes are caused by shifting masses of rock below Earth's surface. The moment magnitude scale, a successor to the Richter scale, measures the amount of energy (or magnitude) released by an earthquake.

Moment Magnitude Scale

Magnitude	Effects	Estimated Frequency
2.5 or less	Usually not felt, but can be recorded by seismograph.	900,000 each year
2.5 to 5.4	Often felt, but only causes minor damage.	30,000 each year
5.5 to 6.0	Slight damage to buildings and other structures.	500 each year
6.1 to 6.9	May cause a lot of damage in very populated areas.	100 each year
7.0 to 7.9	Major earthquake; causes serious damage.	20 each year
8.0 or greater	Great earthquake; can totally destroy communities near the epicenter.	One every 5 to 10 years

Did you know?

A magnitude 7.0 earthquake releases an amount of energy equivalent to 25 atomic bombs.

Most Extreme Earthquakes

Rank	Location	Year	Magnitude
1	Chile	1960	9.5
2	Prince William Sound, Alaska	1964	9.2
3	Sumatra - Andaman Islands	2004	9.1
4	Honshu, Japan	2011	9.0
5	Kamchatka, Russia	1952	9.0
6	Arica, Peru (now Chile)	1868	9.0
7	Cascadia Subduction Zone	1700	9.0
8	Offshore Chile	2010	8.8
9	Off the coast of Ecuador	1906	8.8
10	Rat Islands, Alaska	1965	8.7

MEGAQUAKE HAITI!

The Day the Earth Ransacked an Island

On January 12, 2010, a magnitude 7.0 earthquake struck the Caribbean island nation of Haiti. Homes, government buildings, hospitals, and schools were destroyed. According to official estimates, the earthquake killed 316,000 people, injured 300,000, and displaced 1.3 million people.

Haiti is one of the poorest nations in the Western Hemisphere and has been slow to recover. In the years following the quake, hundreds of thousands of Haitians lived in temporary tent cities where they were forced to cope with inadequate access to water, poor sanitary conditions, and a cholera epidemic.

Did you know?

The 2010 earthquake in Haiti was the second deadliest earthquake in history.

Date: January 12, 2010
Location: Haiti
Magnitude: 7.0
Fatalities: 316,000
Damage: $13.2 billion

VOLCANOES
CHAOS ERUPTS FROM BELOW

A Chain Reaction

After decades of dormancy, the Nevado del Ruiz volcano in Tolima, Colombia erupted on November 13, 1985, catching nearby towns unprepared. Hot ash and magma melted snow and ice on top of the mountain. The resulting lahars (mud and debris flows caused by volcanic eruptions) buried the city of Armero and killed 23,000 people.

Since 1982, volcanic eruptions have been given a number 0 to 8 on the Volcanic Explosivity Index (VEI) based on how much volcanic material is spewed out, to what height, and how long the eruption lasts. The 1985 Nevado del Ruiz eruption was given the classification VEI 3.

Did you know?

While the 2010 eruptions of Eyjafjallajökull in Iceland were relatively small, they majorly disrupted air travel in parts of Europe.

Earth Shattering Eruptions

Rank	Event	Location(s)	Year	Fatalities
1	Mount Tambora (Year Without a Summer)	Indonesia	1815	100,000
2	Krakatau	Indonesia	1883	36,000
3	Mount Vesuvius	Pompeii and Herculaneum, Italy	79 AD	33,000
4	Mount Pelée	Martinique	1902	29,000
5	Nevado del Ruiz (Armero tragedy)	Colombia	1985	23,000
6	Mount Unzen	Japan	1792	15,000
7	Mount Kelud	Indonesia	1586	10,000
8	Laki	Iceland	1783	9,350
9	Santa Maria	Guatemala	1902	6,000
10	Mount Kelut	Indonesia	1919	5,115

LANDSLIDES
EARTH'S ROUGH EDGE

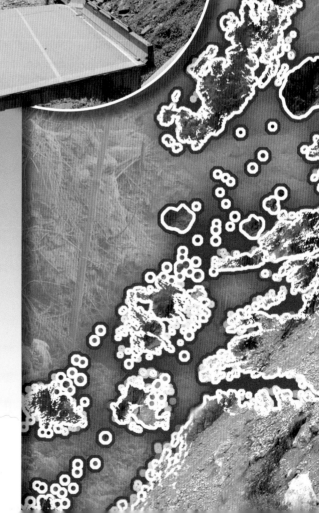

A Slippery Slope

Thousands of people die in landslides each year. Landslides occur when rock, earth, or debris moves down a slope and are often caused by other natural disasters. Volcanic eruptions, earthquakes, hurricanes, excessive rainfall or snowmelt, and soil erosion can trigger landslides.

The magnitude 7.9 earthquake that struck in Sichuan Province, China on May 12, 2008 triggered colossal landslides. Hundreds of landslide dams were formed, blocking rivers and causing backed up water to flood. The 2008 landslides claimed thousands of lives and damaged or destroyed millions of homes in Sichuan Province.

CAUTION

Lethal Landslides

Rank	Location(s)	Year	Cause	Fatalities
1	China	1920	Earthquake	100,000+
2	Venezuela	1999	Rainfall	30,000
3	Pakistan and India	2005	Earthquake	25,500
4	Colombia	1985	Volcanic eruption	23,000
5	China	2008	Earthquake	20,000
6	Peru	1970	Earthquake	18,000
7	Honduras, Guatemala, Nicaragua, and El Salvador	1998	Rainfall	10,000
8	Tajikistan	1949	Earthquake	7,200
9	Peru	1941	Dam failure	4,000 to 6,000
10	Indonesia	1919	Volcanic eruption	5,110

Did you know?

Debris flows can travel down slopes at speeds up to 200 miles per hour.

DROUGHTS

THE PLANET'S DRY SPELLS

Extreme Lack of H_2O

When water is scarce, it can have a huge impact on the environment, agriculture, economy, and the people in the affected region. Droughts kill crops, livestock, livelihoods, and people all over the world.

One of the worst droughts in U.S. history parched much of the Midwest and Northern Plains in 1988. Rainfall totals were between 50 and 85 percent below normal. The forest fires that accompanied the 1988 drought burned 4.1 million acres of land, including more than 700,000 acres of Yellowstone National Park.

The 1988 drought was the costliest in U.S. history, with damages totaling $40 billion ($77.6 billion in today's dollars).

Palmer Drought Severity Index

The Palmer Drought Severity Index (PDSI) uses rainfall and temperature information to measure dryness.

4.0 or more	Extremely wet
3.0 to 3.99	Very wet
2.0 to 2.99	Moderately wet
1.0 to 1.99	Slightly wet
0.5 to 0.99	Incipient wet spell
0.49 to -0.49	Near normal
-0.5 to -0.99	Incipient dry spell
-1.0 to -1.99	Mild drought
-2.0 to -2.99	Moderate drought
-3.0 to -3.99	Severe drought
-4.0 or less	Extreme drought

EMERGENCY BURN ADVISORY

DROUGHT CONDITIONS

USE EXTREME CAUTION

THE DUST BOWL
NATURE'S BIG BACKLASH

Giant Clouds of Dirt

In the 1930s, drought hit the Southern Plains. The area around the Oklahoma panhandle was hit hardest. Farmers there had plowed up millions of acres of native grasslands to make room for crops such as wheat, stripping the land of its natural protection against soil erosion and drought.

Dust storms picked up the topsoil and blew it eastward, leaving behind near desert conditions. Huge dust clouds blackened the sky, hurt crops, killed livestock, and made people sick. So much dirt blew out of the Southern Plains that the region and era became known as the Dust Bowl.

Did you know?

Some dust storms, or "black blizzards," traveled as far as Washington, D.C., and New York City.

Years: 1931-1939

Locations: Texas, Oklahoma, Nebraska, Colorado, and New Mexico

Acres affected: 100 million

Causes: Drought, farming practices, soil erosion, and wind

The Dust Bowl's worst dust storm, called **"Black Sunday,"** struck the Oklahoma and Texas panhandles on April 14, 1935. The black blizzard made airborne more than 300,000 tons of topsoil.

BLIZZARDS
SUPERCHARGED SNOW

You're Gonna Need a Bigger Shovel

In March 1993, the "Storm of the Century" clobbered the eastern coasts of Canada, Cuba, and the United States. Twenty states from Alabama to Maine reported snowfall totals in the double digits. The blizzard dumped an incredible 60 inches of snow on Mount Le Conte in Tennessee's Smoky Mountains. More than 200 hikers had to be rescued. Georgia, North Carolina, Tennessee, and Maryland set all-time statewide records for deepest snow during the 1993 storm.

Storm of the Century

Snowfall total	Location
60 inches	Mount Le Conte, Tennessee
50 inches	Mount Mitchell, North Carolina
44 inches	Snowshoe, West Virginia
43 inches	Syracuse, New York
36 inches	Latrobe, Pennsylvania
29 inches	Page County, Virginia
24 inches	Mountain City, Georgia
20 inches	Chattanooga, Tennessee
18.2 inches	Asheville, North Carolina
17 inches	Birmingham, Alabama

Did you know?

The difference between a blizzard and a snowstorm is wind strength. A snowstorm must have sustained winds of over 35 miles per hour to be considered a blizzard.

Worst Winter Storms in the U.S.

Rank	Storm	Year	Fatalities
1	Great Blizzard of 1888	1888	400
2	Great Appalachian Storm	1950	353
3	Storm of the Century	1993	300
4	Great Lakes Storm	1913	250
5	Children's Blizzard	1888	230
6	Armistice Day Storm	1940	154
7	Knickerbocker Storm	1922	98
8	Blizzard of 1999	1999	73
9	Superbowl Blizzard	1975	70
10	Cleveland Superbomb	1978	70

AVALANCHES
SNOWSLIDES ON STEROID

Not Just a Few Flakes

An avalanche can occur whenever there is a mass of snow and a slope for it to slide down.

On February 26, 1910, a heavy snowstorm stranded a passenger train carrying 119 people in the tiny town of Wellington, Washington. Passengers slept on the train as crews tried to clear the tracks. On March 1, a wall of snow crashed down the mountain, killing 96 people in what was the worst avalanche in United States history.

Many avalanche-prone areas now have barriers to prevent such disasters. Rescue dogs can help find people buried under snow after an avalanche.

Did you know?

Worldwide, approximately one million avalanches happen each year. Europe's Alpine region suffers more avalanches than anywhere else in the world.

World's Worst Avalanches

Rank	Avalanche	Location	Year(s)	Fatalities
1	1970 Huascarán Avalanche	Yungay, Peru	1970	20,000 to 80,000
2	White Friday Avalanche	Italian-Austrian Alps	1916	10,000
3	1962 Huascarán Avalanche	Ranrahirca, Peru	1962	2,700 to 4,000
4	Rodi Avalanche	Plurs, Switzerland	1618	2,427
5	Winter of Terror	Swiss-Austrian Alps	1950-1951	265
6	Blons Avalanches	Blons, Austria	1954	200
7	LaHaul Valley Avalanche	LaHaul Valley, India	1979	200
8	Salang Avalanches	Afghanistan	2010	165
9	Wellington, Washington Avalanche	Wellington, Washington	1910	96
10	Galen Avalanche	Rhone Valley, Switzerland and France	1720	88

SINKHOLES
DEVOURING FROM BENEAT

Watch Where You Step

Sinkholes can swallow up cars, houses, trees, and people in a matter of seconds. On February 28, 2013, a man fell into a sinkhole that suddenly opened beneath the bedroom of his home in Seffner, Florida. Florida is especially prone to sinkholes because the ground there contains a lot of limestone and other carbonate rock, which gradually get eaten away by groundwater. This forms holes underground that collapse when the rock can no longer support the weight of what is above it.

Did you know?

In China, a sinkhole is called a tiankeng, which means "heavenly pit."

Famous Sinkholes

Name	Location	Famous Fact
Qattara Depression	Egypt	Largest natural sinkhole in the world; covers 7,000 square miles
Xiaozhai Tiankeng	China	Deepest sinkhole in the world; more than 2,100 feet deep
Devil's Sinkhole	Texas	Home to millions of bats
Sarisariñama Sinkholes	Venezuela	Contain plant and animal species found nowhere else on Earth
Great Blue Hole	Belize	Largest underwater sinkhole; 984 feet across and 410 feet deep

THUNDERSTORMS
THE LOUDER SIDE OF LIGHTNING

Time to Hide Under the Covers

Thunderstorms produce deadly lightning and are usually accompanied by gusty winds, heavy rain, and sometimes hail. The thunder that follows a flash of lightning is caused by lightning bolts, which create sound waves. We see lightning before we hear thunder because light travels faster than sound.

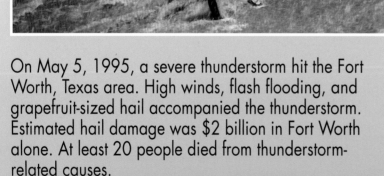

On May 5, 1995, a severe thunderstorm hit the Fort Worth, Texas area. High winds, flash flooding, and grapefruit-sized hail accompanied the thunderstorm. Estimated hail damage was $2 billion in Fort Worth alone. At least 20 people died from thunderstorm-related causes.

Did you know?

Worldwide, there are an estimated 16 million thunderstorms each year.

Stormiest Cities in the U.S.

Rank	City	Average number of annual thunderstorms
1	Fort Myers, Florida	89
2	Tampa, Florida	87
3	Tallahassee, Florida	83
4	Gainesville, Florida	81
5	Orlando, Florida	80
6	Mobile, Alabama	79
7	West Palm Beach, Florida	79
8	Lake Charles, Louisiana	76
9	Daytona Beach, Florida	75
10	Vero Beach, Florida	75

LIGHTNING
THE LIGHTER SIDE OF THUNDER

You See It Before You Hear It

Lightning starts within storm clouds. An electrical charge builds up inside the cloud and is then discharged with a flash of lightning between the cloud and the air, between two clouds, or between the cloud and the ground. A bolt of lightning can travel at speeds up to 8,700 miles per second and be even hotter than the surface of the Sun.

The area between Tampa and Orlando, Florida, is called Lightning Alley because every year in that area there are more than 50 strikes per square mile. The Congo Basin in Africa has twice as many lightning strikes as Florida.

FLORIDA

Orlando

Lightning Alley

Tampa

Did you know?

Lightning strikes Earth more than 8 million times a day—that's 100 times every second.

Average temperature of a bolt: 40,000°F to 50,000°F
Average length of a bolt: 2.5 miles
Average speed of a bolt: 224,000 miles per hour
Average electricity in a bolt: 100 million volts

Most Struck States

Rank	State	Average number of cloud-to-ground flashes per year
1	Texas	2,892,486
2	Florida	1,383,228
3	Oklahoma	1,034,890
4	Missouri	1,026,432
5	Kansas	910,740
6	Louisiana	909,274
7	Mississippi	866,997
8	New Mexico	854,227
9	Alabama	821,365
10	Arkansas	799,034

METEORS
GALAXY SPACE PEBBLES

It's Not a UFO

A meteor streaking across the sky is a beautiful sight. But when a meteor collides with Earth, the result is not so pretty.

On February 15, 2013, a meteor exploded over the city of Chelyabinsk, Russia. The meteor entered the atmosphere at an estimated speed of 40,000 miles per hour, generating shock waves that shattered windows and injured more than 1,000 people. Meteorite fragments left several impact craters behind. The meteor strike was the largest since the Tunguska event of 1908, which flattened an estimated 80 million trees in a remote area of Russia.

Did you know?

A meteoroid in space becomes a meteor when it enters a planet's atmosphere. Pieces that survive and hit the surface are called meteorites. If an asteroid enters an atmosphere, remnants that hit the surface are also called meteorites.

Meteor Crater Rd

Meteor Crater
Natural Landmark →

Notable Impact Craters

Name	Location	Estimated diameter
Vredefort Crater	Free State, South Africa	236 miles
Chicxulub Crater	Yucatán, Mexico	106 to 186 miles
Sudbury Basin	Ontario, Canada	81 miles
Woodleigh Crater	Western Australia, Australia	25 to 75 miles
Manicouagan Crater	Quebec, Canada	62 miles
Acraman Crater	South Australia, Australia	56 miles
Chesapeake Bay Crater	Virginia, United States	53 miles
Gosses Bluff Crater	Northern Territory, Australia	1.8 miles
Barringer Crater	Arizona, United States	0.7 mile

GALACTIC MEGASTORMS
ALIEN WEATHER REPORTS

And You Thought We Had Megastorms

Earth is not the only planet that churns out megastorms. Gas giants Jupiter, Saturn, Neptune, and Uranus have massive, hurricane-like storms that last for years. Mars has huge dust storms and tornado-like dust devils.

Jupiter's Great Red Spot is a hurricane more than twice the size of Earth—the largest storm in the solar system. In 2010, scientists found a storm on Saturn called a Great White Spot that stretched some 65,000 miles. Neptune boasts some of the solar system's strongest winds, which can whip around the planet at speeds more than 1,200 miles per hour.

Jupiter's
great red spot

Saturn's
great white spot

Neptune's
great dark spot

Mars
dust storm

Did you know?

Mars is home to the largest known volcano in the solar system, Olympus Mons, and one of the largest impact craters, Hellas Planitia.

Planetary Storms

Name	Location	Fact
Great Red Spot	Jupiter	Has been raging continuously for at least 300 years
Great White Spot of 2010	Saturn	Largest of Saturn's periodic Great White Spot storms
Great Dark Spot of 1989	Neptune	Spun counterclockwise and moved westward at almost 750 mph
Little Red Spot	Jupiter	About the same size as Earth with 400 mph wind speeds
Martian Dust Storm of 2001	Mars	Biggest global dust storm on Mars in decades

SURVIVAL TIPS
YOUR LIFE MAY DEPEND ON THE[M]

Be Prepared

When Mother Nature wreaks havoc, you may have only seconds to react. Know the risks in your area and pay attention to the warning signs. Plan ahead and keep calm.

Emergency kit supplies:

- Water
- Non-perishable food
- Weather radio
- Flashlight with extra batteries
- Bandages and first aid supplies

First Aid Kit

Tornadoes

Go to the basement, cellar, or a smal[l] windowless interior room or hallway in the lowest floor of a sturdy building

Hurricanes

Secure your home and evacuate whe[n] the order is given. Stay inside and away from windows and glass doors.

Tsunamis

An earthquake may mean that a tsunami is coming. Move uphill and inland, away from the coast.

TSUNAMI
EVACUATION
ROUTE

Floods

Turn around before you drown! Even a few inches of fast-moving water can carry people and cars away.

Rip currents

Swim parallel to the shore until the current weakens, then swim to shore. If you cannot escape, float or tread water.

Thunderstorms

When thunder roars, go indoors! There is no safe place outdoors during a thunderstorm.

Blizzards

Seek shelter immediately. The risk of frostbite and hypothermia increases every minute you are exposed.

Avalanches

Keep a hand in front of your mouth to make a pocket of air. Try to get a hand above the snow so rescuers can find you.

Earthquakes

Drop, cover, and hold on. Stay clear of anything that might fall on you.

Meteors

With early detection, giant meteors may be deflected or blown up before they strike Earth.

Volcanoes

Stay inside. Save water in your bathtub and other containers—supplies may become polluted.

Landslides

During intense rainfall, move quickly if you hear unusual sounds like trees cracking or boulders knocking together. Save yourself, not your belongings.

Always take notice of any warning signs posted.

GLOSSARY

Avalanche: A large mass of snow and ice sliding down a mountainside or over a cliff.

Blizzard: A severe winter storm with sustained winds over 35 miles per hour.

Cyclone: A hurricane-like storm occurring in the South Pacific or Indian Oceans.

Flash flood: A sudden and destructive surge of water, often caused by intense rainfall.

Hurricane Warning: Issued when hurricane conditions are expected in an area in 36 hours or less.

Hurricane Watch: Issued when hurricane conditions with sustained winds greater than 74 miles per hour are possible in an area within 48 hours.

Lahar: A mudflow that occurs on the slopes of a volcano.

Landslide: The sudden and rapid downward movement of rock, earth, or debris down a steep slope.

Landslide dam: A natural damming of a river of some kind by a landslide, debris flow, or volcano.

Magma: Extremely hot molten rocks deep within Earth.

Meteor: A space rock that has entered a planet's atmosphere.

Meteorite: A piece of a meteor or asteroid that hits the surface.

Palmer Drought Severity Index: Uses information about rainfall and temperature to measure dryness.

Rip current: A narrow, powerful current of water that runs from the beach out into the ocean.

Saffir-Simpson Scale: Uses wind speed determine the intensity of a hurricane.

Seismic wave: A wave of energy caused by an earthquake or another Earth vibration.

Sinkhole: A hollow place or depression in which drainage collects.

Storm surge: A wave of water several feet in height created by a severe storm that washes over shorelines.

Tornado Warning: Issued when a tornado has been actually sighted or indicated by weather radar; seek shelter immediately.

Tornado Watch: Issued by the National Weather Service when tornadoes are possible i your area; stay tuned to radio or television new

Tsunami: A giant wave or series of waves triggered by an earthquake, volcanic eruption, landslide, or meteorite impact.

Typhoon: A hurricane-like storm that forms over the Western Pacific Ocean or China Sea.

Volcano: An opening in Earth crust from which melted or hot rock and steam come out.